COPING WITH
ILLNESS

Liz Miles

www.raintreepublishers.co.uk
Visit our website to find out more information about Raintree books.

To order:
☎ Phone 0845 6044371
🖷 Fax +44 (0) 1865 312263
✉ Email myorders@raintreepublishers.co.uk

Customers from outside the UK please telephone +44 1865 312262

Edited by Louise Galpine and Laura Knowles
Designed by Richard Parker
Original illustrations © Capstone Global Library Ltd 2011
Picture research by Liz Alexander
Originated by Capstone Global Library Ltd
Printed and bound in China by South China Printing Company Ltd

ISBN 978 1 406 21987 6 (hardback)
14 13 12 11 10
10 9 8 7 6 5 4 3 2 1

ISBN 978 1 406 21994 4 (paperback)
15 14 13 12 11
10 9 8 7 6 5 4 3 2 1

British Library Cataloguing in Publication Data
Miles, Liz.
Coping with illness. -- (Real life issues)
155.9'16-dc22
A full catalogue record for this book is available from the British Library.

Acknowledgements
We would like to thank the following for permission to reproduce photographs: © CCA p. 30; Alamy pp. 9 (© Paul Doyle), 13 (© Lisa F. Young), 43 (© PhotoAlto), 34 (© Spencer Grant); Corbis pp. 6 (© Dr. Gopal Murti/Visuals Unlimited), 21 (© FEDERICO GAMBARINI/epa), 26 (© Peter Turnley), 28 (© Beau Lark), 35 (© Image Source); Getty Images pp. 7 (Colin Hawkins/Cultura), 10 (Elliot Elliot/Johner Images), 15 (Brent Stirton/Getty Images for the GBC), 27 (Jose Luis Pelaez Inc/Blend Images); Photolibrary pp. 8 (Image Source), 12 (Corbis), 16 (Denis Meyer/imagebroker.net), 20 (ERproductions Ltd/Blend Images), 24 (Juice Images), 37 (Comstock), 19, 23; Press Association Images p. 41 (Fiona Hanson/PA Wire/PA Archive); Science Photo Library pp. 17 (Paul Rapson), 33 (Coneyl Jay), Shutterstock pp. 5 (© Monkey Business Images), 39 (© maga).

"Distressed texture" design detail reproduced with permission of iStockphoto/© Diana Walters.

Cover photograph of a worried boy lying on a bed reproduced with permission of Photolibrary/Image Source.

Quotation on page 14 extracted from Surya Bhattacharya, 'Orphans of AIDS: Missing out on your childhood', *Faze Magazine* (Issue 20), www.fazemagazine.com. Quotation on page 17 reproduced by permission of Connect with Kids. For information, visit www.connectwithkids.com.

We would like to thank Anne Pezalla for her invaluable help in the preparation of this book.

Every effort has been made to contact copyright holders of material reproduced in this book. Any omissions will be rectified in subsequent printings if notice is given to the publishers.

In order to protect the privacy of individuals, some names in this book have been changed.

CONTENTS

Stay safe on the internet!

When you are on the internet, never give personal details such as your real name, phone number, or address to anyone you have only had contact with online. If you are contacted by anyone who makes you feel uncomfortable or upset, don't reply to them, tell an adult, and block that person from contacting you again.

Any words appearing in the text in bold, **like this**, are explained in the glossary.

Introduction

Most of us have felt unwell at some time. Perhaps you have had a bad cold, or something more serious. Illness is part of our lives, and it is important to know how to cope with it.

Every illness is different

Many illnesses, such as a sore throat, pass quickly without treatment. Other illnesses, such as **cancer**, are serious and need treatment. Some illnesses are there from birth, while others are caught as infections or appear for complicated reasons. Any part of the body can become ill, from ears to stomachs. Many illnesses are invisible to us, for example **disorders** of the brain.

Carers

Carers look after people who are ill and help them to cope. Some are specially trained, but many carers are simply the partner, parent, child, or other relative of the patient. They have to learn a lot about the patient's needs, and must know when to ask for help.

Coping

Whether it is you or someone you know who is ill, coping during these times can be difficult. This book suggests ways of coping. It is important to ask for help when you need it. There are many well-trained people who can provide support. You can find organizations that can help you on pages 46–47.

Some hospitals are specially for children and young adults. The staff enjoy helping young patients.

Online!

There is a huge amount of information about illnesses on the internet. However, every illness affects people differently. If you are ill, it is best to ask your own doctor any questions. Remember that information on the internet can be inaccurate. Have an adult help you work out which websites are reliable.

What is illness?

Illnesses range from mild to serious. Mild illnesses usually come and go, and are not difficult to cope with. Other illnesses have to be treated by trained people, such as doctors.

Common cold

The common cold is the illness that affects us most. On average, children catch six to ten colds a year. The symptoms can include coughing, a runny nose, and headache. There are over 200 **viruses** that can cause a cold. A healthy body can fight a cold virus so that the cold usually disappears after seven to ten days. Although the symptoms are uncomfortable, a cold is not difficult to cope with. A bad cold might make you want to stay in bed. Some people take medicines such as painkillers to help them feel more comfortable.

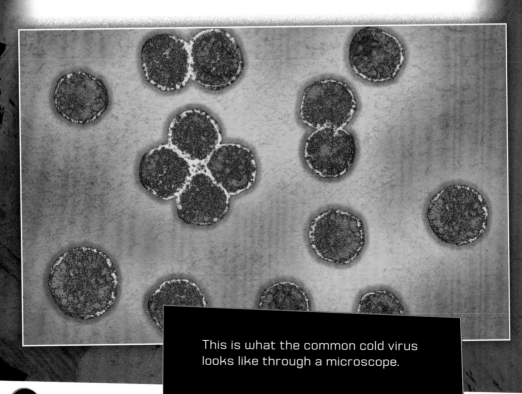

This is what the common cold virus looks like through a microscope.

Staying at home

If you are feeling ill, it can sometimes be best to stay at home. If there is a chance that you could make other people ill, you should stay at home until you feel better. This will help reduce the chance of you passing your illness on to others.

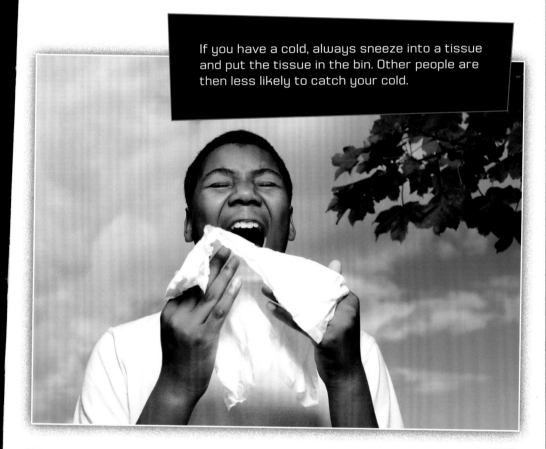

If you have a cold, always sneeze into a tissue and put the tissue in the bin. Other people are then less likely to catch your cold.

CASE STUDY

Oliver, aged 9, remembers having a bad cold and feeling too ill to go to school and needing to rest. "I stayed at home and kept warm. I could not do anything, so lay on the sofa. I even had to turn off the television as the flashing colours made my head feel weird."

Long-term illnesses

Some illnesses are **long-term** and can even last a lifetime. Long-term illnesses include **asthma** and autism. Understanding a long-term illness is the first step in coping – whether you are the sufferer or the friend or relative of a sufferer.

Asthmatic friend

Asthma sufferers may need to inhale a medicine to help them breathe. An understanding friend will make sure they give them the space and time to do this.

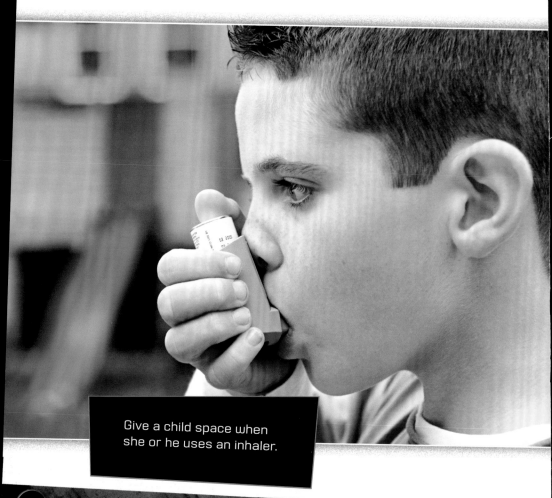

Give a child space when she or he uses an inhaler.

Understanding autism

Children with autism can have problems communicating and fitting in. They might find it hard to see other people's points of view. An autistic child might:

- not meet your eye
- not want to play with other children
- get upset by loud noise and cover their ears.

Before **diagnosis**, people sometimes wrongly think an autistic child is being naughty because they do not follow instructions and get upset easily. Scientists think that children with autism have slightly different brain structures to non-autistic children.

CASE STUDY

Understanding what it means to be autistic can make you more sensitive and caring towards those with autism. Charlie, aged 9, has a brother, aged 7, who is autistic. Charlie describes his brother: "He doesn't like being touched. He wants to dress the same as me. I have to keep an eye on him on the road to make sure he's safe. At school, he has a teaching assistant to help him. Sometimes people ask him if he wants to play but he doesn't want to join in. Sometimes when he's angry he hits himself on the head. He can be a bit annoying, like when he likes touching people's wobbly teeth or mosquito bites."

Autism is described as an "invisible disability" because you cannot always tell if someone has it when you meet them.

Life-threatening illnesses

Some illnesses are very serious and need urgent treatment. Life-threatening illnesses can bring an end to a patient's life. However, if they receive treatment, a patient can cope and live for many years. For example, a patient who has a major **heart attack** might have an operation on their heart. Without the operation, the patient could die. After the operation, they will probably be able to live a fairly normal life.

Terminal illness

Some illnesses are so serious that they are described as terminal. Sadly, this means that the patient will die. Doctors can rarely predict how long it will take for a patient to die from a terminal illness. A dying person needs lots of care. If you know someone who is dying it is important to talk about your feelings. Many people are afraid of death because they don't know what it will feel like. Other people may not feel sad about dying at all. They may have led a happy life and are content with the idea of dying.

People who are very ill usually love to have visitors.

BEHIND THE HEADLINES

Scientists are always searching for ways to cure illnesses. Recently scientists have begun to make new organs using a patient's own **stem cells**. In 2009 a 10-year-old boy was given a new trachea (windpipe) created from his own stem cells. The trachea he was born with was too narrow for him to breathe. With the new trachea, the boy was able to breathe normally.

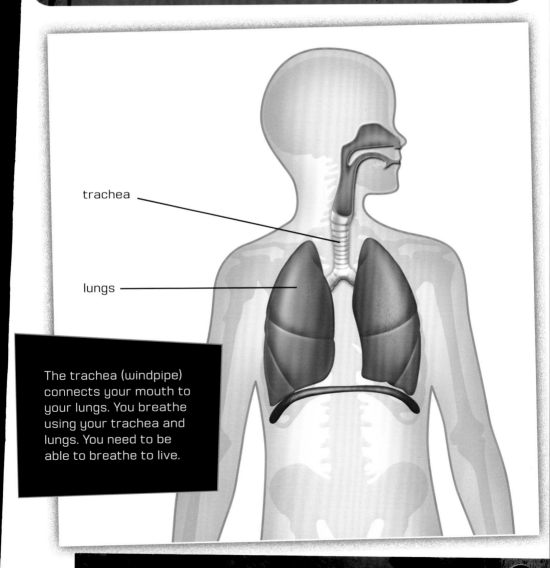

trachea

lungs

The trachea (windpipe) connects your mouth to your lungs. You breathe using your trachea and lungs. You need to be able to breathe to live.

Who is affected?

Anyone can be affected by illness, and a person can become ill at any time in his or her life. However, some people are more vulnerable (likely to develop an illness) than others. This group includes babies and older people.

Babies

Some babies are born with an illness or condition. Often it is not serious, and the baby will be kept in hospital for just a few days. If it's more serious, they may be put in an incubator. This is a closed-in cot that keeps the baby warm and helps him or her to breathe. It can be a worrying time for parents, brothers, and sisters.

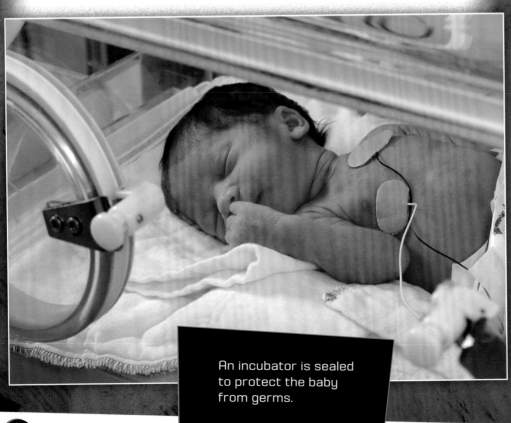

An incubator is sealed to protect the baby from germs.

Older people

Older people often suffer from illnesses. As bodies age, they become frail and parts wear out. Older people may need more care and help at home. Families often try to help the oldest members of their family.

Arthritis is the common name for conditions that make the joints and bones painful. In older people, a wearing away in the joints can make walking painful. If it is serious, they may go to hospital for an operation. The surgeon puts in a replacement hip or knee joint.

Older people sometimes need help with everyday tasks.

BEHIND THE HEADLINES

Many people were frightened when a new type of flu spread around the world in 2009. It was called swine flu because it was thought to have started in pigs. Most people who catch it get better after a few days. However, vulnerable people, such as children under 5, adults over 65, and people suffering from certain illnesses, can die from swine flu. Many countries quickly tried to get their most vulnerable people **vaccinated**.

Caring for a parent

Illness also affects the people who live with or know the patient. Some children have to look after their parents. Thousands of children under 18 years old help to look after a parent or other relative at home. Many get help from professionals, such as nurses, but in some cases, there is no other adult at home to help. Children as young as 5 help to look after people with physical and mental disabilities. Always remember that there is support for young carers (see the websites on pages 46-47). The help ranges from ideas on how to keep up-to-date with your homework, to contacts for extra help at home.

Orphans in Africa

A disease known as **AIDS** is a serious problem in some African countries. AIDS is caused by a **virus** called HIV. This virus has spread rapidly across Africa because many countries are too poor to provide health education to teach people how to protect themselves against it. The lack of money means that medicines are in short supply too. In South Africa alone, 1.4 million children have become orphans because of AIDS. The illness caused the deaths of their mothers and fathers. Older relatives often look after the children.

CASE STUDY

An article by Faze Magazine tells the story of 13-year-old Patience, who lives in a village in Zimbabwe. "Patience lost her mum six years ago, and her dad abandoned the family when Patience's mum first fell ill … Two years ago, when her aunt was unable to feed her, Patience started living on her own, surviving on support from a local community group … She is able to afford only two meals a day." There are many charities you can support to help children like Patience cope.

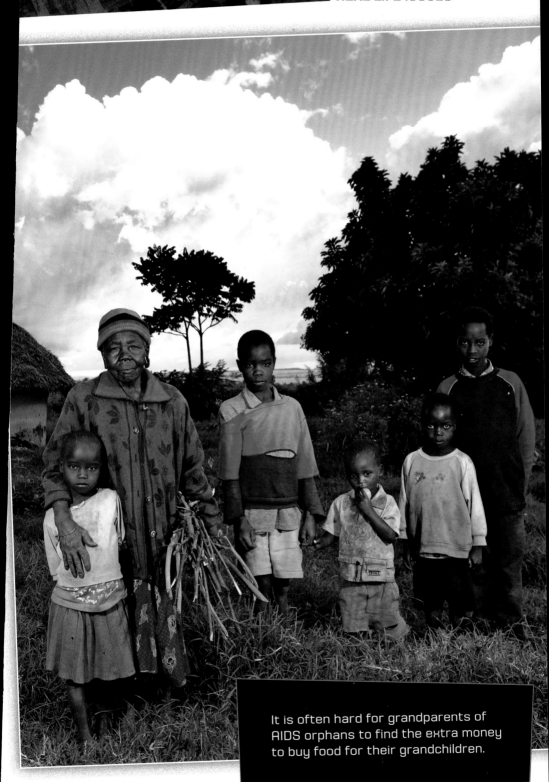

It is often hard for grandparents of AIDS orphans to find the extra money to buy food for their grandchildren.

Finding out what is wrong

If you feel unwell, in pain, or as though something is wrong with a part of your body, it is important to tell your parents. They may take you to a doctor, who will usually be able to work out what the problem is. If the doctor is unsure, he or she might suggest some tests.

Simple tests

Most tests are simple, quick, and don't hurt at all. Sometimes a sample of your blood is sent to a **laboratory**, and the results come back in a few days. Blood samples can tell the doctor if organs and glands are working properly.

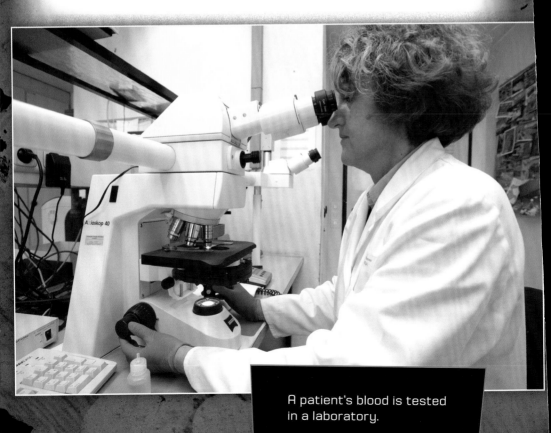

A patient's blood is tested in a laboratory.

BEHIND THE HEADLINES

It has been reported that 4–8 per cent of children are affected by food allergies, and the numbers are increasing. An allergy is when the body reacts to a normal food type as if it is harmful. Symptoms include dizziness, vomiting, and rashes. Tests find out which foods the child is allergic to, so that they can be avoided. Only eight foods cause 90 per cent of food allergies. They are cow's milk, eggs, peanuts, nuts from trees (such as walnuts), fish, shellfish, soybeans, and wheat.

A scratch test will show which food a person is allergic to.

CASE STUDY

It is important to know what to avoid if you have a serious allergy. Some people suffer from life-threatening symptoms, such as not being able to breathe. Jeff, aged 10, is allergic to peanuts, and even the smell of them sets off a reaction. Jeff says: "my throat swells up and my lips swell too and I have trouble breathing."

Hospital tests

Some tests are done in clinics or hospitals, using special equipment. These tests include the use of heart monitors to check that the heart is beating correctly and **X-ray** machines that show images of bones and organs inside the body.

Scans

A CT scanner is a special X-ray machine that gives very detailed images of parts inside the body, such as the brain. A person lies in a CT scanner while rays are aimed at his or her body. The person has to keep very still, but it does not hurt.

Biopsies

A **biopsy** is carried out in hospitals and clinics. Sometimes lumps appear in women's breasts or other parts of the body. These need to be checked to make sure they are not **cancerous**. A sample of the lump is taken and sent to a laboratory. If the result shows the lump is **benign** (not **cancer**) everyone is relieved. If it is **malignant**, that means the lump is cancerous and has to be removed.

CASE STUDY

Anna's stepmother found a lump on her breast. The lump was removed and tested. Anna, her stepmum, and her dad were worried about what the results would be, but the doctor explained that most lumps (80 per cent) are benign. Even if the lump was malignant, most women are free of breast cancer for the rest of their life after treatment, especially if the lump is found and treated soon after it appears. A few days later they got the result: benign. It was a relief for the whole family.

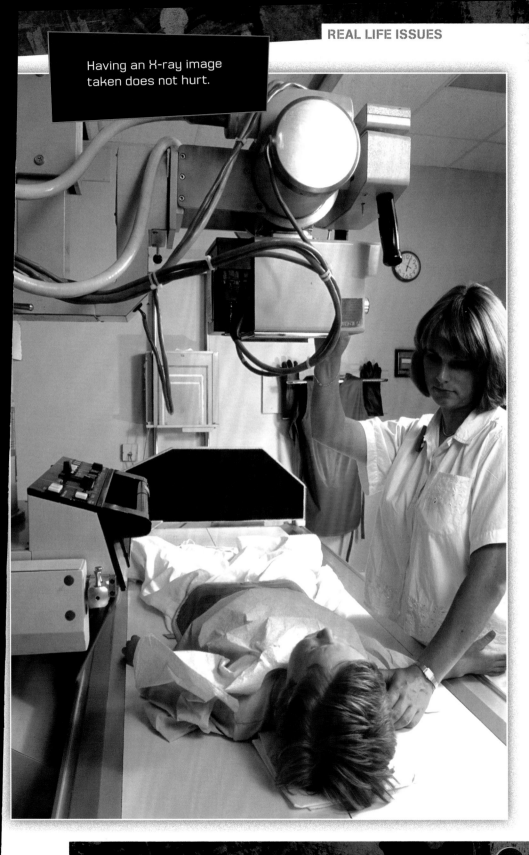

Having an X-ray image taken does not hurt.

Going to hospital

Most people first go to their doctor if they are ill. The doctor asks questions, examines the patient, and carries out simple tests. Doctors will often listen to your heart and use equipment to examine your eyes, nose, or throat.

Sometimes it is necessary for a person to go to hospital. A visit can be for just a few hours, or longer with overnight stays. People go to hospital, or a clinic, for all kinds of reasons. Here are a few:

- emergency care, such as after an accident
- further tests to find out what is wrong
- an operation, or surgery
- special medical treatment, such as **chemotherapy**
- **counselling**.

Urgent treatment is available in Accident and Emergency departments of hospitals.

A&E

If you have an accident you will be taken to the Accident and Emergency department (A&E). A relative might take you in a car, or an ambulance might take you. The doctors and nurses treat the most seriously ill patients first. They will be kind and caring.

Hospitals around the world

Hospitals in many countries, such as the United Kingdom, United States, and Australia, are usually comfortable, clean, and have good equipment. Unfortunately, hospitals can be quite different in poorer countries, and especially after a natural disaster, such as an earthquake.

BEHIND THE HEADLINES

On 12 January 2010, an earthquake destroyed buildings and killed and injured many people in Haiti, a country in the Caribbean. Hospitals were soon overcrowded. Many people, including children and babies, had to lie on the floor or outside on the ground. There were not enough doctors or equipment.

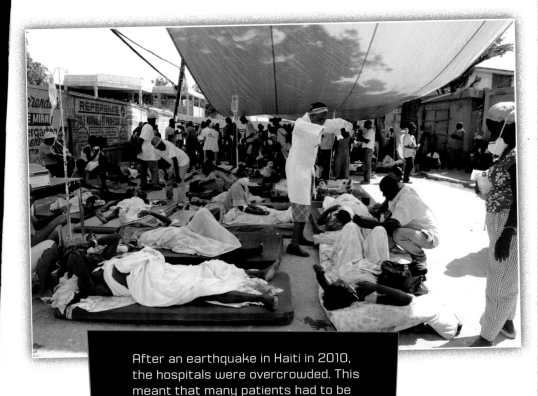

After an earthquake in Haiti in 2010, the hospitals were overcrowded. This meant that many patients had to be treated outside.

Staying overnight

You may have to stay overnight in a hospital. It might seem scary at first because it is different to what you are used to, but you will soon feel happier and comfortable. The friendly staff will look after you. Children have special wards of their own. Children's wards are usually colourful, with plenty of books and games, and a television so you do not get bored.

CASE STUDY

Suna, aged 9, remembers the best things about her stay in hospital: a television with films, a playroom, delicious food, and two lovely nurses.

The people you meet

Going to hospital is serious, but there are ways to make it fun. You will meet other children who are ill. Some will be well enough to talk or to play; others will not. You will also meet people who do interesting jobs. Some of these are:

- nurses – they work with doctors and make sure your stay is comfortable
- consultants – these doctors know a great deal about certain illnesses
- surgeons – they perform the operations.

Online!

You can find out what it is like to stay in a hospital by looking at children's hospital websites on the internet. The Kids First for Health website (see page 46) lets you know what you can expect during your stay.

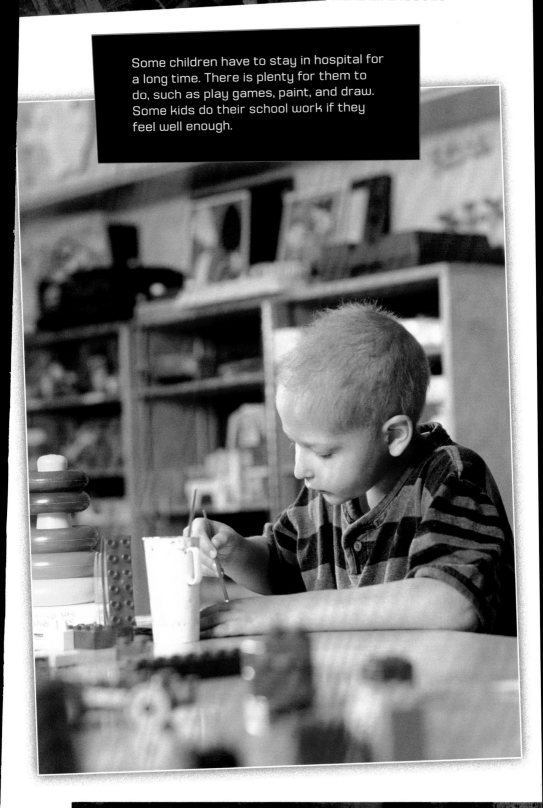

Some children have to stay in hospital for a long time. There is plenty for them to do, such as play games, paint, and draw. Some kids do their school work if they feel well enough.

Operations

You may have to go to hospital for an operation. Some people are frightened, but the nurses and doctors will make sure you are comfortable. Your parents will be able to stay with you most of the time.

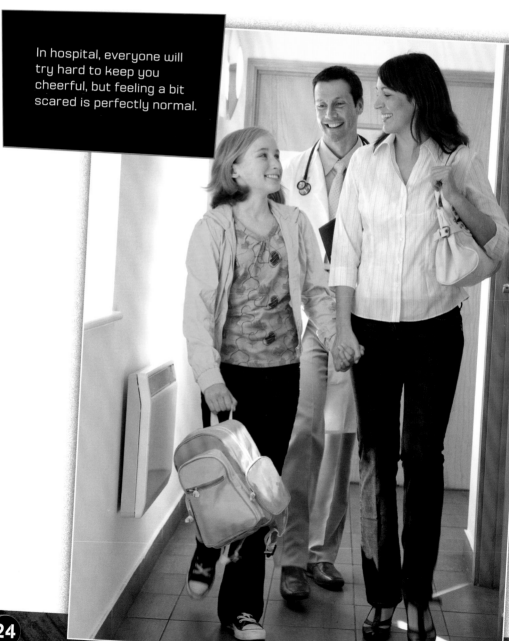

In hospital, everyone will try hard to keep you cheerful, but feeling a bit scared is perfectly normal.

Feeling numb

For most operations you will have a general anaesthetic, which stops you feeling any pain and makes you go to sleep. For some treatments, such as having a bad cut stitched up, you will have a local anaesthetic. This numbs only a part of the body and you are still awake while you are being treated.

Before ...

You may go to a pre-op appointment before an operation. The staff will tell you all about what is going to happen and you can ask any questions you like. If you are having a general anaesthetic you will not be allowed to eat for a few hours before the operation. Before being taken to the operating theatre you might be given a pre-medication. This will stop you feeling worried or scared.

... and after

After it's all over you will wake up in a recovery room, where the nurses will keep a close eye on you. You will feel tired, perhaps a bit sick, and sore. Soon you will be taken back to the ward, where you can rest until you feel well again.

CASE STUDY

George, aged 8, went into hospital for an ear operation. He said, "I saw a nurse before the operation who told me what would happen. ... My mummy came to theatre with me and was in the recovery room when I woke up. I had bandages over my ears, so did my teddy. I felt a bit sick but soon felt fine." Overall, George said, "it was a good experience, but going home was my favourite bit!"

Prevention and treatment

We need to take care of our bodies to help prevent illness. For example, we should eat the right foods, in the right amounts.

Every day in the world, 16,000 children die from hunger-related illnesses. People in poorer countries, such as Somalia, often suffer from **starvation** (lack of food) when there is no food available. In richer countries **obesity** is a problem because of **high-fat foods** and because many people do not do enough exercise. In the United States, a survey showed that 17 per cent of children aged 2–19 years are obese. Obesity can lead to life-threatening illnesses, such as high blood pressure and diabetes.

Starvation stops the body from working properly.

WHAT DO YOU THINK?

Should companies be allowed to sell fast food that is high in fat, even though it could lead to obesity?

Yes, they should	No, they shouldn't
Companies should be allowed to sell what they like. Customers can choose not to buy unhealthy food.	Companies should be made to take the temptation away.
Some people like fast food. It is okay to eat it occasionally.	Children can get used to the taste of high-fat foods and want too much of it.

What causes obesity?

Obesity is not always caused by overeating or eating the wrong sorts of food. It can be caused by things such as stress, genetics, and a low **metabolism**. If you are overweight, it is probably a good idea to lose weight. But before you try, you must ask a doctor how to lose weight safely.

Unfortunately, obese children and adults are sometimes bullied. This makes things far worse. Bullying should never happen, so if you or someone you know is being bullied, tell a parent or teacher.

Eating the wrong kind of foods can lead to obesity and life-threatening illnesses.

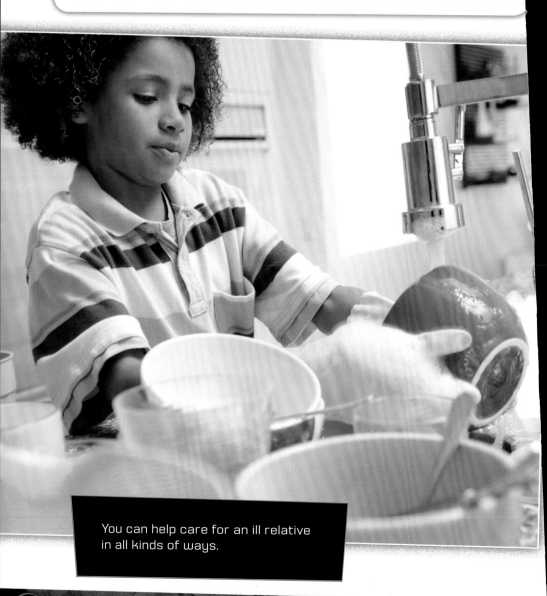

You can help care for an ill relative in all kinds of ways.

Talking

When people are ill, they often have to be cared for at home by relatives or friends. **Long-term** illnesses can mean many years of hard work. If you have a relative at home who is seriously ill, you will feel all kinds of emotions. You might feel upset, worried, or even angry. It is important to talk to people about how you feel. Find someone you can trust at home or at school, or ring a **helpline** (see pages 46–47). Remember that usually illness is not anyone's fault.

Hospital care

Some accidents can leave people severely **disabled**. For example, brain damage can change their lives forever. The patient may never be able to go home from hospital. If you have a relative who is in hospital long-term, you will probably visit them. To make the most of your visits, plan them in advance. Think of interesting, happy things to say. Take something to show, such as photographs.

Online!

Seventeen-year-old Sophie Wilkinson was in a tragic car accident. Her brain was so badly damaged that she has been in a **vegetative state** ever since. She needs full-time care from hospitals and her family. You can visit the Sophie's Gift website to find out how the family care for Sophie and how they are thanking Sophie's hospital.

Treatments

It helps to remember that many new treatments are becoming available, including new drugs and technology. New treatments mean that people are surviving with diseases that they would have died from not long ago.

Five-year-old Eli Walker suffers from a type of cancer called leukaemia. In 2009 he was named a Community Hero by the Children's Cancer Association for his courage in battling the disease.

Kicking cancer

Cancer is a disease in which cells grow and divide too much and can start to destroy the body. There are more than 200 different types of cancer. Cancer treatments are often successful today. With the right treatment, most patients can beat cancer.

CASE STUDY

Judy was told she had a type of cancer known as Hodgkin's disease when she was 14 years old, and had never heard of the illness before. She was very, very ill. After a month of tests, she had 12 **chemotherapy** treatments. Her hair fell out (but later grew back). She missed a lot of school. But 8 months after she first became ill, she had an **X-ray**. She was thrilled to be told that the cancer was gone. Judy is now in her 30s and cancer free, and has three children of her own.

Online!

Research into curing diseases, such as cancer, is important. Many charities are involved in raising money for research and offering support to patients. Even if you don't know someone who has had cancer, you might like to get involved in raising funds for a charity. Look for fundraising events on the internet, such as at the Children's Cancer Research Fund, Race for Life, and Cancer Research UK websites.

Fears and worries

We all like to fit in and be accepted by our friends. It can be difficult if we become ill because it makes us feel different. It is important to talk about any worries you might have. Talking helps you work things out and lets other people help you.

CASE STUDY

Judy (see page 31) wants ill children to learn from her experience and to be open about how they feel. She wishes she had talked more to family and friends when she was ill. She wishes she had told them she was afraid.

Being normal

Some illnesses force people to do things that others don't have to do. Thousands of children suffer from type 1 diabetes. People with this illness have problems with their pancreas, an organ in their body. Their pancreas does not make enough **insulin**. This means they are unable to make use of glucose (sugar) from food. People with type 1 diabetes have to inject insulin into their bodies to do the job. They also have to eat healthy meals at planned times, and check their sugar levels.

If you have type 1 diabetes it is important to explain the illness to your friends. A teacher or parent will help you. Once people know, you won't feel so embarrassed or different.

Online!

If you have diabetes, ask a parent to look for diabetes **support groups** on the internet (see page 46 for a website address). Talking to other children with diabetes can help with any worries or fears. You will get tips on how to cope with the illness, and how to explain it to people.

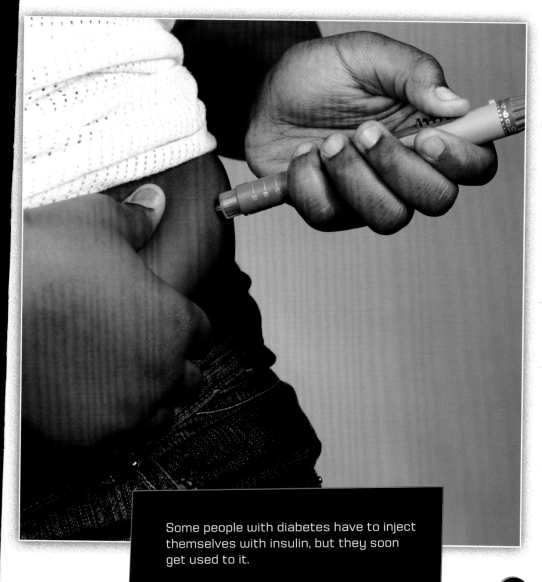

Some people with diabetes have to inject themselves with insulin, but they soon get used to it.

33

Mental health

Mental health problems and **disorders** cause all kinds of fears and worries. You may know someone who behaves in an unusual way, which can be frightening. But if you learn about their problem or disorder, your fears will probably change into sympathy and understanding.

ADHD

Attention-deficit **hyperactivity** disorder (called ADD or ADHD) is one of the most common chronic (ongoing) conditions suffered by children. In the United Kingdom, around 5 to 10 per cent of children and teenagers are thought to be affected by the condition. ADHD makes it difficult for children to control how they behave, to sit still, pay attention, or concentrate. ADHD is not anyone's fault.

The more a teacher knows about ADHD, the better they will be able to support pupils who have the condition.

Help

If you have ADHD, you may be given medicine, taught how to relax, or go to see a therapist. A therapist will help you plan tactics to make life easier. If you know a child with this problem, try to help them. Never be cruel or call them names.

If you know someone at school who has ADHD, don't distract them during work time. This will make it easier for them to concentrate.

Online!

If you suffer from a mental health problem, try reading other people's life stories. You might pick up some tips on how to cope. Telling your own story can help too. Writing everything down makes things clearer and less scary. Keeping a journal or blog online can really help. You can both read and share at the Young Minds website (see page 47 for details).

Talking it over

Many children suffer from anxiety or sadness, but these feelings are usually nothing to do with mental illness. However, children who do suffer from a **mental disorder** should get professional support and help. Talking about the problem is the first step to feeling better.

Whether you are ill or not, if you are sad or upset, angry, or frightened, it is important to talk about your feelings to people you trust. Talk to a relative, teacher, doctor, or a professional on a helpline.

Helplines

Around the world there are helplines for children that offer professional help and advice. Helplines are anonymous, which means that nothing you say will be passed on. The person who answers will not be surprised or embarrassed by anything you say, as they are likely to have spoken to people with similar problems before. You can find the helplines on the internet (see pages 46–47).

Express yourself!

Expressing your feelings is important. Talking to people is one way to do this. Perhaps painting a picture can be a way of expressing your feelings, too. If you are angry, play a sport, or even shout into a pillow.

Mental health problems can be treated with support, counselling, and sometimes medicines. Talking openly about these problems is important.

Eating disorders

People with severe eating **disorders**, such as **bulimia** and **anorexia**, may not realise they have these illnesses. This means it is very important to support sufferers. If you think you suffer from an eating disorder it is important to tell someone you trust.

Warning signs

It is sometimes hard to know for certain if you, or someone you know, has an eating disorder. Early signs include:

- a major change in eating habits, such as not eating the food on a plate
- thinking your body or parts of it are large when they aren't
- an obvious loss of weight or obvious changes in weight.

If you notice some of these signs in a friend, ask an adult for advice on what to do.

CASE STUDY

If you do know someone who has an eating disorder, you can find ways of helping them on the internet. At The Beat website (see page 46) you can read about Becky's ideas on how to support a sufferer, and the things to keep in mind if you talk to them. Her ideas include:

- Even though someone is getting better, it doesn't mean they won't have difficult times. Don't give up on them – support them and help them get back on the road to recovery.
- Recovery takes time – be patient.
- Give them time and listen to what they have to say. Do what you can to help them, but look after yourself at the same time, too.
- Don't abandon them. With help and support, they can get better again.

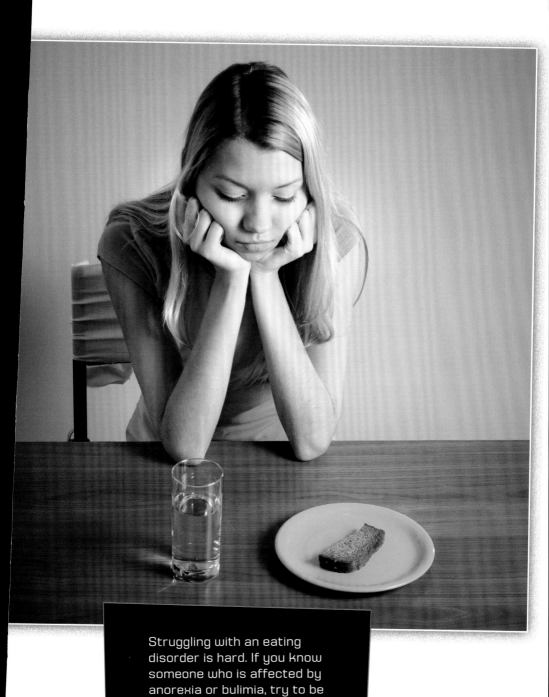

Struggling with an eating disorder is hard. If you know someone who is affected by anorexia or bulimia, try to be sensitive and supportive.

Coping together

Coping with the illness of yourself or others can feel scary and unfair. However, illness can also help to bring people together. Everyone becomes ill at some time in his or her life. People are eager to support and help each other when they feel unwell.

Caring for others

The best way to cope with someone's illness is to find out about the illness. You will then be better able to understand how the person is feeling. Being caring and thoughtful will help the person to feel better. If you feel upset, talk to someone. You must look after yourself as well as others!

Caring for yourself

If you are ill it is important to ask for help. Friends, family, and professionals will be happy to offer advice. If you would rather ask for help or advice from somebody who doesn't know you, you can ring a helpline (see pages 46–47).

If you go to see a doctor, or go to hospital, it is important to do what the medical staff suggest. Everything they say and ask you to do is because they want you to get better.

BEHIND THE HEADLINES

In 2006 six-year-old Mollie and her four-year-old brother Cameron's lives suddenly changed. Their mother, Wendy, was **diagnosed** with **cancer**. The children wanted to take care of her so that their dad, David, could carry on working. Every day they had to wash, dress, and make breakfast for their mum. In 2009, Mollie and Cameron were given a Children of Courage award for caring for their ill mother and for coping so well.

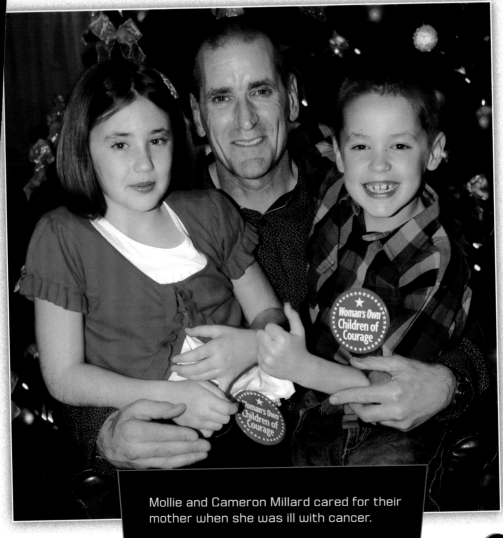

Mollie and Cameron Millard cared for their mother when she was ill with cancer.

Top ten tips for coping with illness

If you or others around you are facing illness, you might feel helpless. Here is a list of things to remember to help you cope and beat the illness:

1. Find out about the illness. Don't be afraid to ask questions. Medical staff are the best sources of information.

2. Don't be afraid to talk about how you feel. Everyone feels different emotions at different times. It is better to talk about them with someone you trust and not bottle them up.

3. Share your experiences with people who are going through the same sort of thing. There are **support groups** for most illnesses and support groups for carers.

4. Follow instructions from medical staff if you are unwell. They are trying to help you, so it is polite to be helpful, too.

5. Be sensitive towards people who are ill. Don't ask them questions or mention the illness unless you are sure they want you to.

6. If you are ill, remember that your family and friends will be worried for you. Sometimes they will show that they are worried, sometimes they will hide it.

7. Don't talk about a person's illness without thinking first. Remember that some things are private. If you want to pass on personal information, ask permission first.

8. If someone is ill, try to be positive. If they become angry or upset, remember that it is not your fault. They will be going through all sorts of emotions.

9.   Remember that an illness isn't anyone's fault. Nobody can be blamed for getting ill, and nobody makes people ill.

10.   Keeping a diary is a good way of coping with illness. If you are ill, or you know someone who is, write down how you feel and what happens.

If you are ill, talking about how you feel can help.

Glossary

AIDS serious condition that is caused by a virus called HIV

anorexia (anorexia nervosa) mental health condition that makes a person want to avoid eating

asthma disease that affects the tubes that carry air to and from the lungs and makes breathing difficult

benign type of growth that has no signs of cancer. A benign growth is mild and less likely to harm your health.

biopsy removal of tissue (cells) under the skin which is then tested

bulimia (bulimia nervosa) mental health condition that causes a person to overeat and then vomit

cancer disease when abnormal cells grow in the body

cancerous linked to the disease cancer. For example, a cancerous growth is a growth caused by cancer.

chemotherapy special drugs that are used to treat diseases such as cancer

counselling meeting with a trained person who can talk through problems with you, giving you information and advice

diagnosis working out what disease a patient has

disabled unable to do something, such as behave or move in a certain way

disorder when something, such as the brain, is not working properly

heart attack when the heart suddenly stops working properly. This is very dangerous, and the person must receive medical help right away.

helpline telephone service offering advice. Helplines are often free.

high-fat food food that contains a lot of fat, such as cheese, butter, and fatty meats. Too much fat is bad for your health.

hyperactivity working unusually hard or fast. Hyperactive children find it hard to concentrate. Some illnesses are caused by a hyperactive gland in the body.

insulin chemical that controls how much sugar is in a person's blood

laboratory room where scientists use special equipment to do things such as blood tests or examine cells taken from patients

long term for a long time. A long-term illness may remain for months or even years.

malignant type of growth caused by the disease cancer. A malignant tumour often gets worse and can spread, causing serious health problems.

mental disorder repeated ways of thinking or behaving in a person which makes him or her suffer and not always be able to live a normal life

metabolism process through which food is broken down in the body

obesity condition of being very overweight

starvation extreme hunger due to a lack of eating essential foods

stem cell cell that can renew itself or multiply, making new body tissue

support group people who gather together and talk because they share a common experience, such as an illness like diabetes

vaccinated when a "mock" germ has been put into the body. This gets the body to produce defences, in case the real, harmful germ invades.

vegetative state describes a patient with brain damage who is unaware of their surroundings

virus microscopic creature that feeds inside the cells of other creatures; viruses cause illnesses such as colds, mumps, and AIDS

X-ray special type of photograph that shows the bones and organs inside the body

Find out more

Books

Health (Go facts: Healthy Bodies), (A&C Black, 2010)

Health (Our Rights), Katie Duckworth (Evans, 2008)

Health and Disease (Headline Issues), Sarah Levete (Heinemann Library, 2010)

Hospital (Separations), Janine Amos (Cherrytree Books, 2008)

Illness (Tough Topics), Ana Deboo (Heinemann Library, 2008)

Illness and Injury (Healthy Kids), Sylvia Goulding (Cherrytree Books, 2006)

Websites and organizations

The following organizations and websites can offer help, support, and information for you and your family:

www.b-eat.co.uk
Visit this website for information on eating disorders, how to get help, and what you can do to help someone you know who has an eating disorder.

www.childline.org.uk
Telephone: 0800 1111
ChildLine has trained counsellors who give advice, support, and information on a range of issues. Calls are free and won't appear on the phone bill. Visit their website to find out how to email their counsellors or chat to them online. You can also write to ChildLine at Freepost 1111, London, N1 0BR (no stamp needed).

www.childrenfirst.nhs.uk/kids
Kids First for Health is an NHS website that gives information on how to keep healthy, different illnesses and conditions, what it's like visiting hospital, and much more.

www.childrenscancer.org/stories-of-hope/kids-stories
Visit this website to read kids' stories about beating cancer.

www.childrenwithdiabetesuk.org
This website will help you and your family get in touch with
other children with diabetes.

www.sophies-gift.org
This website tells about Sophie Wilkinson's life, her hospital care,
and what her family are doing to raise money to buy lifesaving
equipment for her hospital.

www.youngcarer.com
Local support groups around the United Kingdom can be found
at this site for young carers.

www.youngcarers.net
Young Carers Net is a charity supporting young carers in the
United Kingdom. The website is packed with helpful information,
advice, support, and recreational activities designed to give
young carers time out. There are also case studies and chatrooms.

www.youngminds.org.uk
For help about how you feel, and for information on mental
disorders, see the Children's section of this website. To read about
other young people's experiences, click on 'My Head Hurts' and
then 'Real Life Stories'.

www.winstonswish.org.uk
Telephone: 08542 03 04 05
Winston's Wish offers help and support for children living with a
family member who has a serious illness.

Index